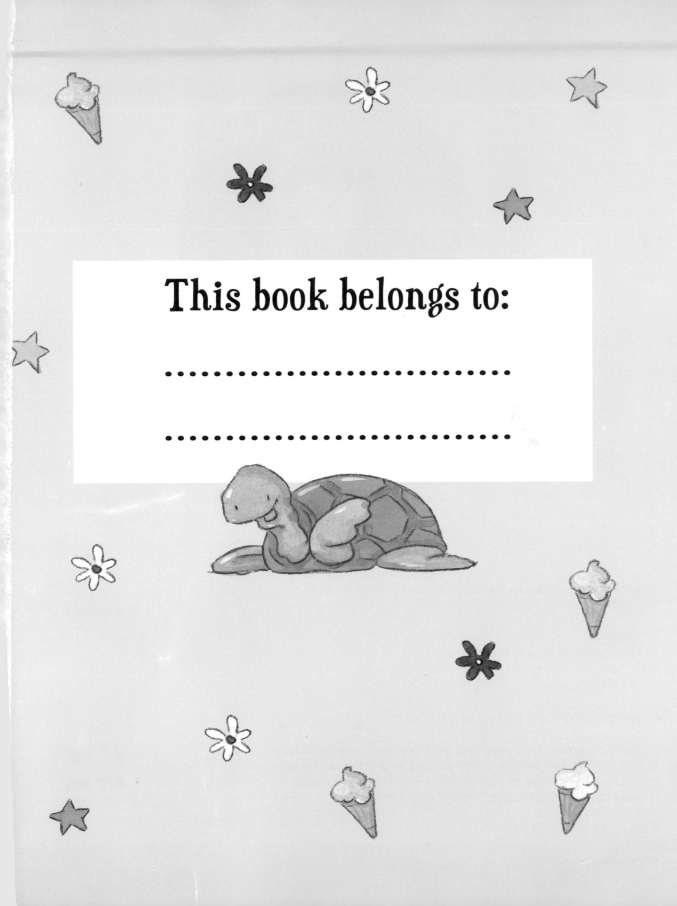

This book belongs to:

....

....

Written by Jillian Harker
Illustrated by Rachael O'Neill

This edition published by Parragon Books Ltd in 2015
and distributed by

Parragon Inc.
440 Park Avenue South, 13th Floor
New York, NY 10016
www.parragon.com

ISBN 978-1-4748-0342-7

Printed in China

Let's Share!

Bath · New York · Cologne · Melbourne · Delhi
Hong Kong · Shenzhen · Singapore · Amsterdam

Mind your child's manners!

It's important to start teaching good manners early so they become a habit for life. The stories in the MIND YOUR MANNERS! series are written to make learning good manners a positive experience.

Here are some of the ways you can help to make it fun:

* Find a quiet time to look at this story together and encourage your child to join in. The rhymes make the story easy to remember.

* After every question, talk about what you might say or do. Ask your child for suggestions. Joining in will help them to learn.

* Use the pages at the end of the story to check that your child understands when it is appropriate to use good manners. There's a reward star for every right answer.

* Throughout the day, reward your child's good manners with plenty of praise—and a colorful sticker.

"That looks fun!
Can I play, too,
And share your
bouncy ball with you?"

"I will share my ball with you. Sharing's fun!

"Playing is more fun with two!"

"That looks fun!
Can I paddle, too,
And share your cool
tide pool with you?"

"I'll share my pool with you.

"Paddling is more fun with two!"

"That looks fun!
Can I dig, too,
And share your
shovel and pail with you?"

"I'll share my shovel and pail
with you,

"Digging is more fun with two!"

"That looks good!
Can we share, too,
And eat your picnic
snack with you?"

Let's
share

"No!
I don't want to share my
picnic with you!"

How rude!

"Oops! Sorry, I forgot,

"You've all shared with me a lot.

"I would love to share with you,

"Sharing's much more fun to do!"

What will you do?

When someone asks to join your game, what will you do?

If you said "Let's share," you were right!

When someone asks to share your special place, what will you do?

If you said "Let's share," you were right!

Did you say "Let's share" in all the right places?
Then give yourself a star!

When someone asks to play with your toy, what will you do?

If you said "Let's share," you were right!

When someone asks to share your food, what will you do?

If you said "Let's share," you were right!